How to remember
EVERY DAY
of your life

About the author

SIDNEY CHAN was born in Sydney, Australia. As he moved to Hong Kong before the age of one, Cantonese became his mother tongue instead of English. When he started studying in England at the age of 17, he arrived with basic English but quickly became dedicated to reaching fluency. Following his A-levels, Sidney completed a Veterinary Medicine degree at the Royal Veterinary College in London.

Sidney has always sustained a wide range of interests and his determined nature has meant he isn't content until 'mastering' each of them. Creativity is the core value of his life and he especially enjoys painting and playing / composing music (piano, violin, flute and saxophone). On the geekier side, he also indulges himself in solving Rubik's cubes and keeping his mind busy with memory sports. Languages are also a strong interest of his; one of his life goals is to be able to comprehend written texts as well as a native in 10 languages (currently working on French, Italian and German).

Travelling and meeting new people also adds colour to his life. He joined Mensa in 2017 to meet others with similar aspirations. He believes that living is somewhat similar to memory forming by synapses - the more connections you make between people and places, the more meaningful and interesting your life experience will be.

Home in Hong Kong, 2010

'Wow! It actually works!'
Brian Chan, Managing Director

'I wasn't sure if I could do this, it seemed too hard, but I am reaching a month now!'
Lottie Perry, Secondary School Student

'Interesting read. Would definitely recommend it to my friends!'
Clementine Paine, Veterinary Nurse

'Genius idea. Every day means so much more to me now.'
Ekie Mak, University Student

'How precious that I can now easily remember my little boy's special moments and firsts.'
Gemma MacKenzie, Mother

How to remember
EVERY DAY
of your life

A step-by-step tutorial to creating a Mental Diary

Written by Sidney Chan

Cover design and artwork by Sidney Chan

First Printing in 2018

ISBN 978-0-244-98675-9

Independent Publishing Body
Chan's Memory Office 16714, PO Box 7169
Poole, BH15 9EL

remember.every.day.of.your.life@gmail.com

*For anyone who would like to
remember a bit more*

Imagine, 2012

Contents

Foreword

What do you think 'forgetting' actually means? For me it doesn't always mean that you have 'lost' the memory. Indeed, I think most of the time when we think we have forgotten something, it is in fact still there. I believe that a better way to describe it is 'I am not presently able to locate it in my memory archive'.

My interest in the art and sport of memory started during my final exam period of vet school. This was when a close friend of mine introduced to me the ancient memory technique of **Memory Palace** (known as the Method of Loci) [1]. It completely blew my mind, because it took little time and effort to learn but worked like magic. It was intended to help me with revision, but I went off track and became distracted by other memory techniques instead! One of the most useful ones I came across was converting digits to images, which enabled me to memorise any shuffled deck of cards in under 5 minutes after a few days practice; I had found my genuine brain hack. The great thing is that everyone is capable of learning these techniques. Every day, I ask myself - why wouldn't more people want to know about it? And why aren't students taught this at school? Perhaps the latter is not the best suggestion, given that **memory sports** [2] diverted my concentration away from my final exam!

I hope my story is interesting enough to keep you reading... if not, please still have a look at some of the questions I pose in the next chapter, maybe this will change your mind! I am aware that plenty of people (especially in the Memory Sporting community) may have already attempted to reach the goal of 'remembering every day' using their own methods, but I don't think there is any published literature available. Thus, this is the reason I've written this book. Finally, in case you are wondering, I did pass my exams in the end!

Ripples, 2016

First of all, why?

Why would you want to do it?

Pause and think… What was the most memorable thing that happened to you in the past month? You may be able to recall a good number of events because they happened not long ago. But what about in the past 6 months, 12 months or in the past few years? You might notice that there are less things you can think of per period the further back you explore. Imagine how amazing it would be if you could pick a random date and be able to immediately recall what you did with your friends, what happened in the news, or even what you had for dinner.

Remembering every day has proven to me its practical value: over time you will remember numerous peoples' birthdays with ease; new peoples' names will stick from the day you first meet them; you will know when your car was last serviced so you know when the next one should be; when and why you upset your girlfriend last time so you can avoid making the same mistake (!); when you last signed an important contract; when your boss took a day off unjustly so you can 'remind' him next time he says no to your holiday application etc.

Personally, I also want to make every day *count*, however mundane it may seem to another person. Remembering every day of my life creates an illusion that my life passes more slowly, because every day now seems to be ten times more significant; see it as finding a way to appreciate my time being alive as much as possible. Furthermore, it lights up the connections between people and events. Did you know Stephen Hawking passed away on the same day as Einstein's 139th birthday as well as Pie (π)

day? Did you know Prince William and Princess Kate's son, Louis, was born on the same date as Shakespeare's birth and death? I have also gained appreciation from my family and friends for remembering moments that mean something special to them.

Equally, people have long been speculating how exercising your brain can have various benefits, such as improving cognitive performance [3] and delaying its functional decline [4]. The fact is, no one has shown that our memory actually has a limit. Personally, I don't believe that it does. Whether that is true or not, in my mind, there is no reason why we shouldn't maximise the use of our brains and keep them active.

What does it mean to remember 'every day' of your life?

There are a handful of people in the world who are said to have a condition where they remember every day of their life in extraordinary detail, without any effort. This is called hyperthymesia. A few examples have been included for interested readers [5, 6, 7, 8]. However, even these gifted few, are unable to remember every single thing that happens, no one has a perfect memory. Similarly, it is important to note that creating a Mental Diary doesn't suddenly give you 'total' memory, but it is perhaps the closest way you can learn to be like a hyperthymestic and it is definitely achievable. It will allow you to remember A LOT more things, as long as you choose to.

Once the Mental Diary technique is harnessed, it enables you to easily tell what happened on any given date since the start of 'writing'. Equally, you will be able to easily recall which date a particular event took place. This is already significantly much more than most people can do.

My Experience

Having become fascinated by the 'superpowers' of hyperthymestics, I started to wonder - what if anyone could train themselves to do this, to remember every single day? With this aspiration, I started to think of and play around with various methods until, one day I gathered enough ideas to start experimenting with my Mental Diary.

To my surprise, the method has worked very well. Since I started writing my Mental Diary on 16th August 2017, I have remembered the key events of every single day. Now I only regret one thing, that I didn't come up with this idea earlier. I would love to remember my childhood as well as the days I've recorded in my Mental Diary.

Of course it still doesn't grant me a perfect memory, but at least if I am asked what happened on any given date, e.g. 17th November 2017, I'd be able to immediately tell you that on that day we celebrated one of my colleague's birthday at work and that it was Children in Need; a dog with deformed eyelids also had surgery and another colleague punctured her tyre. You can see it was a day that was happy for some, but not for others! If you choose to, you can remember as much detail as you like. If remembering every single day is a skill that I can learn, then I am confident you can too.

How difficult is it and how long will it take?

As cheesy as it sounds, 'No pain, no gain.' One has to understand that a Mental Diary has to be maintained as habit. The longer you have formed it, the stronger you will remember the days. It is likely that the first week after starting your Mental Diary will be your most challenging period, simply because you are new to the method. However, once the habit is formed, it will take a lot less energy and time. Both recalling past days and remembering a new day don't require anything more than the concentration of your mind. Currently, I take about 10 minutes to recall specific diary entries each morning, I usually achieve this while driving to work; every night I mentally write the new day before falling asleep, which takes less than 5 minutes. The more days you have in your Mental Diary, the better you will understand what works best for you, and consequently the easier it will become to maintain your Diary. If you are willing to commit, you will realise that the process of 'remembering' isn't actually tiring, rather it can be incredibly interesting and even rewarding.

How can I do it then?

If I ask you, 'What happened on 20th January 2017?', it is likely that you will be unable to recall any specific details, unless something very significant happened, a birthday or anniversary. On the other hand, if I ask you, 'Do you remember the day when Donald Trump was inaugurated as U.S. president (which happened on 20th January 2017)?', you are much more likely to remember what else you did on that day. The reason this date didn't remind you of Trump becoming president is simple - there was no connection made between the date and its event. This is key when writing a Mental Diary. It is based on the working mechanism of forming an association between any specific date and its corresponding events. As a result, if I ask you what happened on this particular date OR on which date did a major event happen, you would be able to recall immediately and effortlessly.

Yesterday, 2018

Your Goal

Your ultimate goal is to form a **Mental Diary** which helps you to form a link between a *date* and the *events* which happened on that day, so that if you are asked what happened on this particular date, you would be able to tell straightaway. Reversely, if you are asked when this particular event happened, you would be able to tell which date, given that you have marked that particular event in your Mental Diary.

Realistically, it is not possible for anyone, even hyperthymestics, to remember every single detail of every day. Therefore, only events which are personally important or memorable are chosen and memorised.

Dynamic Mental Image (DMI)

A **Dynamic Mental Image** is a short snapshot that you mentally create. It represents the major events that happened on a specific date. A new DMI is formed daily and is the basic unit you use to form your Mental Diary. This process has been broken down into Steps 1 to 4 to demonstrate how it can be achieved.

There is, ultimately, no right or wrong way to form your DMI. As a general rule, the key element that will keep your Mental Diary strong is creativity. Feel free to go wild with your ideas and personalise any part of this method if you see a better adaption.

You may find it a bit overwhelming at first, but don't give up. Forming a Mental Diary is like a toddler learning to walk: Huge effort is needed to take the first step, but the pleasure it brings will pay off the sweat, and will multiply a thousand times more.

Remember… Don't forget to remember!

To dream, 2017

Step 1 - Each month is a person

Assign 1 person of your choice to each month.

One person will represent one month of a year. In other words, each month is a person. The choice of person is entirely yours, e.g. famous people, historic figures, or even fictional characters from films and animations. Because there are 12 months in a year, you will need to set up a list of 12 people who represent one month each.

Each person will then form an association with *every day* within the month. Your aim is to learn the association of people and the months well, so when you think of one, it leads you to the other. This is to help you identify the specific month of the year by thinking of the particular person. It is easiest to learn them one by one as each month passes, rather than attempt to memorise the whole year before you start.

For example:

<u>Year 2018 Theme: Disney Characters</u>

January - Cinderella

February - Aladdin

March - Mickey Mouse

April - Rapunzel

May - Mr Incredible

June - Winnie the Pooh

July - Sully

August - Buzz Lightyear

September - Moana

October - Stitch

November - Cruella de Vil

December - Ariel

It is advisable to use 12 people under a different theme for the following year, as this will make it easier to differentiate between different years when recalling your Mental Diary.

For example:

<u>Year 2019 Theme: Movie Stars</u>

January - Leonardo DiCaprio
February - Jennifer Lawrence
March - Tom Hanks
April - Scarlett Johansson
May - Angelina Jolie
June - George Clooney

July - Tom Cruise
August - Meryl Streep
September - Hugh Jackman
October - Gal Gadot
November - Nicolas Cage
December - Natalie Portman

Using these examples, each month of the year 2018 is associated to the people under the theme, 'Disney characters'. And, any month in 2019 would lead you to think of the group of people under the theme, 'Movie stars'.

More example themes

Here are some further possible themes for you to choose from, or, by all means, create a theme of your own:

Politicians
Presidents
Favourite sportsmen / sportswomen
Artists
Fictional characters from a movie / animation

Remember, it doesn't require any particular reasoning when choosing which theme to use, or choosing which person to assign to which month. As mentioned before, all you need to do is learn and know your people and their month perfectly.

People to avoid

Friends and family members should be avoided because they are likely to already be associated with your daily events. This could confuse you when recalling each day. Moreover, the action word (See Step 2) could potentially create an unpleasant or uncomfortable Dynamic Mental Image (DMI). You will understand this better as you read on.

Daydream, 2017

Step 2 - Each day is an action

Assign an action word to each day.

Each action word of your choice will represent one specific day of *every* month within the same year. Each month's person will perform the specific action you have set for that day.

Just like Step 1, your aim is to learn the association of the day of the month and its action word well, so if you think of one, it leads you to the other. Again, do not think you need to learn the whole month before you start. Simply learn each action word for 'today' as you write your Diary. To start with, you may find it helpful to recall all the action words learnt to date each day. This will speed up your ability to identify each day's word.

Example:

1st	sweep	16th	push
2nd	squash	17th	shout at
3rd	spin	18th	levitate
4th	twist	19th	kiss
5th	chew	20th	elongate
6th	freeze	21st	slap
7th	burn	22nd	bite
8th	crack	23rd	weight-lift
9th	shoot	24th	sniff
10th	flip	25th	flick
11th	kick	26th	shave
12th	punch	27th	smash
13th	regurgitate	28th	tickle
14th	cut	29th	hug
15th	inject	30th	pinch
		31st	scratch

The list on the previous page is only an example. It is completely your choice to replace any of them with other action words of your liking. Obviously, you can also change the order of action words however you like. For me, the number '1' looks like a broom, and therefore I have set it to the word, 'sweep'. However, there are no rules as to how you set the list of words, nor does the pairing need a meaning. To repeat again, all you need is to learn your list well and commit to the connections, so you can recall them straightaway.

Don't mix up similar words!

It is very important that you don't mix up any action words. For example, there is the potential to mix up the 4th **'twisting'** and the 8th **'crack'**, or the 5th **'chew'** and the 22nd **'bite'**. To prevent yourself from confusing any two similar actions or days, you need to be specific with the action words, using a bit of imagination. For example, for 'twist', make sure the person twists an object without breaking it, even if it is something breakable, such as glass or wood. For 'crack', you can make the process brisk and perhaps add a bone-cracking sound effect. Likewise, for 'chew', it could involve a long movement of the jaw versus a quick nip for 'bite'.

Creativity will certainly help when characterising each action to ensure it is distinct; alternatively, you can simply replace the confusing action words with new ones.

A second list of action words for another year

As you start a second year, a second list of action words should be created. This is to help you differentiate between years. If you can come up with enough action words, you could even create a third (fourth, fifth…) list for the forthcoming years.

Example 2:

1st	poke	16th	pull
2nd	lick	17th	polish
3rd	photograph	18th	blow
4th	shake	19th	season
5th	boil	20th	laugh
6th	stroke	21st	spit
7th	laser cut	22nd	juggle
8th	roll	23rd	massage
9th	propose to	24th	sew
10th	perfume	25th	feed
11th	paint	26th	head-butt
12th	iron	27th	electrocute
13th	arrest	28th	squeeze
14th	worship	29th	cry
15th	fry	30th	shower
		31st	whip

At this stage, you may have a rough idea in which direction this method is heading. Please don't be discouraged if it seems like hard work so far, this is because Step 1 and 2 both require memorisation by rote. The next few steps are based on cognitive techniques and an understanding of the process of remembering; they should, therefore, be more interesting to learn!

Wild Ideas, 2009

Step 3 - Picking the 'symbols' of your day

As mentioned previously, it's not possible, even for hyperthymestics, to remember every tiny detail of each day. Therefore, you should ask yourself one question to identify what you want to remember:

What are the most important and memorable events of today that make it different from any other day?

Maybe you went out for dinner with an old friend; received a parcel that you had long been anticipating; had a tummy-ache; got a speeding ticket; celebrated your mother's birthday etc. These events are chosen by you to be included in your DMI because they hold personal significance and are deemed 'memorable' by you. Two people who experience the exact same day may choose very different combinations of things to remember.

Your next step is to choose a '**symbol**' to represent each event within the day. In most cases, a symbolic item is sufficient, as long as it will remind you of the event.

For example:

Event	Symbol
I went to the gym.	dumbell
I had dinner at a steak restaurant.	steak
I paid the electricity bill today.	power socket
It was my wedding anniversary.	wedding ring
I watched an ice age documentary.	frozen television

It is completely your choice what symbol you set for each event. Just bear in mind that your goal is to pick the simplest thing that will be enough to remind you of the event.

A few tips…

If there is an event that happens regularly, it is best to stick with the same symbol for each DMI, e.g. always use a 'dumbbell' if you go to the gym. However, if it is not a regular event, it may be better to choose something more distinctive.

For example, a 'frozen television' was used because the added element of the TV being 'frozen' reminds you that it was an ice age documentary you were watching. A 'television' alone is simply not informative enough.

Picking symbols to represent each event is a part of the process of compressing information and creating an efficient Dynamic Mental Image (DMI). This will be discussed in greater depth in Step 4.

Step 4 - DMI = [person] + [action] + [symbols]

Steps 1 to 3 have prepared us to create a **Dynamic Mental Image (DMI)** of a day. When any single day is being recalled, its DMI will show you a string of symbols which remind you of what happened on that day, somewhat similar to watching a short video clip. In order to create a Mental Diary, a new DMI has to be formed every day.

DMI = [person] + [action] + [symbols of the important events]

A **Dynamic Mental Image (DMI)** acts as a short 'video clip' that shows you the events of the day.

A new DMI is formed every day to write your Mental Diary.

To start building a DMI, you first need to choose a single location or a place that you have been to on that day. This acts as a 'shelf' for storing your DMI. Then you need to have ready the person of the month (Step 1), your action word for the date (Step 2), and the symbols of your day (Step 3). It is time to start integrating them.

Here are two examples of forming DMIs using the example lists of people and action words from Step 1 and 2.

Example 1:

On 1st January, your friends threw you a surprise birthday party at your home, they baked you a delicious lemon drizzle cake.

Chosen location = home
January = Cinderella
1st = sweep
Symbol of the important event = lemon drizzle cake (birthday party)

Therefore, your DMI could be:
Cinderella sweeps a lemon drizzle cake at home.

Example 2:

On 2nd February, I went for a swim in the morning. Later on, I had an argument with my colleague, Steve, at the office over who should be in charge of the new project. In the evening, my girlfriend comforted me by taking me out for dinner at a pizza restaurant.

Chosen location = the pizza restaurant
February = Aladdin
2nd = squash
Symbols of the important events = a pair of swimming goggles (representing swimming), angry Steve (argument), the pizza restaurant (having pizza with my girlfriend)

Therefore, your DMI could be:
At the pizza restaurant, Aladdin is squashing a pair of swimming goggles onto Steve, who is so angry that his face turns bright red.

There are two things that are worth noting from Example 2:

1. The event of 'going to the pizza restaurant' doesn't require a symbol. The location itself will remind you of having pizza with your girlfriend. Angry Steve being there also gives you the hint of why you were at the pizza restaurant.

2. Anger is intangible, but a red face gives a visual clue for the emotion and reminds you that you had an argument with Steve.

Why do we have to place and mix all the symbols in one location?

Having one location allows you to create a DMI for the day in the most efficient way possible, using minimal information which is just enough to remind you of all the chosen events. The key is to form a string of symbols that links the key events together in as concise a way as possible. This compressing process aims to save you time and brain energy.

Sometimes less is more

Remember, your Mental Diary serves its purpose as a brain hacking tool, not a brain replacement. We don't have to be pernickety and note down all details when forming a DMI; this would be too exhausting and time consuming. If you look around mentally, there are often other clues there to help you identify the events. You can do this by recalling what happened the day before or after, or finding out which day it is in the week (see more in 'Tips to spiT').

When should you build your DMI?

It is up to you when you choose to start memorising. If you start at the beginning of the day and build up the DMI as time passes, you are less likely to miss an important event. On the other hand, if you create your DMI at the end of the day, all events have already taken place ready for you to memorise so the process of compressing your DMI will be more straightforward.

More examples of creating DMIs will be included later in the chapter to aid your understanding - See 'Examples'.

Piecing it together, 2009

Step 5 - Recall... Recall...... Recall..............

In order to strengthen your Mental Diary, it is crucial to revisit the days you have remembered. This process is necessary to solidify each day's DMI. If you don't review them, your DMIs will only stay as short term memories and will disappear like a dandelion clock on a windy day. To make your memory of the days long term you need a smart strategy to revise them.

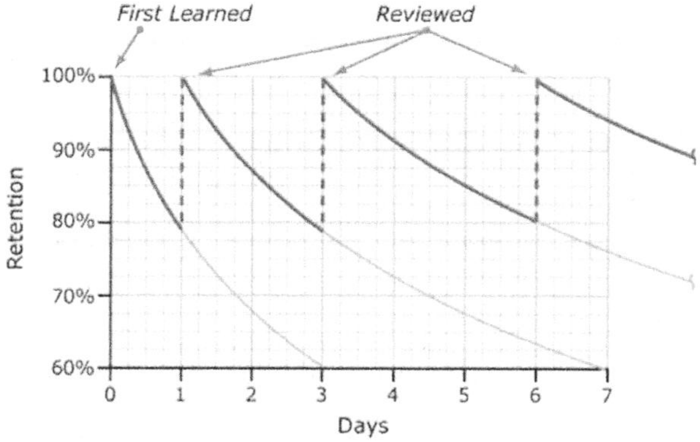

Figure 1. [9]

The German psychologist, **Hermann Ebbinghaus**, suggested that newly learnt information will remain in the memory for longer when it is repeatedly reviewed with increasing intervals; this is known as the Spacing Effect [9]. Figure 1 is a modified version of the '**Forgetting Curve**', it shows that we can slow down the fading of a memory by strategically revisiting them at specific time intervals.

To put this into practical use, I have created a regime for revisiting each day's DMI, systematically revising each day with longer and longer intervals between recalls. The rate of interval increase is carefully measured to prevent the retention of DMIs from dropping too low before the next review but it is also slow enough to allow DMIs to turn into long term memory.

Regime A:

*Review 1 day ago, 3 days, 6 days, 11 days, 18 days, 1 month, 2 months, 3 months, 6 months (1 year, 2 years… etc.)**

**By the time you get to 6 months, the DMIs should be very secure as long term memory, therefore recalling 1, 2, 3 years… is more for interest's sake.*

**But I don't feel confident in my memory v.s.
I think I have a better-than-average memory…**

As Ebbinghaus suggested, the rate of forgetting varies between people. Some may require smaller intervals (more frequent revisiting), whereas others may not need to recall the days so frequently (a faster rate of interval increase). Therefore, if the regime above is either too fast or too slow for you, feel free to set up a regime that you are most comfortable with. You will learn about your pace during the beginning stages of your Mental Diary. Two further examples of regimes are listed below for your reference:

Regime B (if you struggle with Regime A):

Review 1 day ago, 2 days, 3 days, 5 days, 8 days, 13 days, 21 days, 1 month, 2 months, 3 months, 4 months, 6 months, 9 months (1 year, 2 years… etc.)

Regime C (if Regime A's revision is too frequent):

Review 1 day ago, 3 days, 7 days, 14 days, 1 month, 3 months, 6 months, 10 months (1 year, 2 years… etc.)

Monthly and yearly anniversaries

Note that the intervals between revisions don't increase at a constant rate when it gets to 'months' or 'years'. There are three main reasons the regime has been arranged this way:

1. It encourages you to remember accurately each month's person (Step 1), so you don't mix up the same date between months.**

2. Reviewing exactly 1, 2, 3… months or years ago is more meaningful as it marks a monthly / yearly anniversary.

3. It's simply more practical and easy to locate during your revision.

***1st of Jan, 1st of Feb, 1st of March… all share the same action word, therefore there is the potential to mix up different months if you are not careful.*

To prevent this, you can also add characteristics for each person. For example, when I picture Cinderella, there are always birds hovering and whistling songs in the sky around her; every time I imagine Aladdin, he is on his magic carpet floating in the air. You can decide what elements to add to each person to help you best remember. As long as each person is made 'special' enough, it will allow you to better differentiate the same date between different months.

In addition, you can keep the same starting position for each month's person, for example, the person for January may always begin your DMI from the left performing an action to the right.

How do I review / recall a specific day that I have remembered?

Your aim is to be able to retrieve any DMI you have formed for a given date. The process of remembering follows the *same pattern* below every time: (the month people and action words are taken from the example lists shown in Steps 1 and 2)

For example:
What happened on the 4th January 2018?

January, 2018 → Which person is January, under the theme of 2018? (Step 1) → 'Cinderella'

4th → Which action word is it? (Step 2) → 'twist'

Therefore, you know that your DMI starts with [Cinderella] + [twists] + [symbols of events]

The person of the month and the action of the date should already help you bring up the DMI that you constructed for that day, 4th January 2018. You will be surprised how easy it is.

Important notes…

Try to recall the DMI of each day in as much detail as possible. Every day should have a fairly compressed string of events. One easy mistake to make is to omit one of the meaningful pieces. This is usually when symbols are missed, despite the fact that they were clearly placed in your DMI at the time of writing. It is similar to looking for a pair of glasses only to find them on your head, or searching for a lost car key that is in fact held in your hand all the time. It is also important to remember that the chosen location for the DMI always holds an event too.

It may seem strange, but speaking the **events** out loud to yourself when imagining your DMI can be very helpful. It allows you to extract the information from your DMI more thoroughly so you are less likely to miss a symbol. In most cases where you are unable to retrieve a complete DMI, you haven't 'lost' a memory, you have simply forgotten to notice all the symbols that have been deliberately memorised and are meant to be recalled.

Just one more note…

If you are on the last day of the month in February, April, June, September or November, remember to recall the last days of the previous months too. For example, if you are on the last day of November, 30th, reviewing 'one month ago' will bring you back to 30th October, thus you will miss the revision of 31st October.

Lost in Thought, 2007

Tips to spiT

It is completely understandable that you might find this process overwhelming to start with, so here are a few things to help keep everything on track.

Just start and have a go!

You don't have to learn all the action words and months before you start writing your Mental Diary. It will be much easier to learn them one by one as you go on. Writing this Diary is something that you get better at the more you do it.

Start simple

Don't overwhelm your DMI with too many symbols to start with. Picking 1 to 2 symbols in the early days will allow a more gentle introduction. As the days pass, you will find it easier to fit in more and more symbols each day.

What should I do if I really can't remember a specific day / its DMI?

You should really encourage yourself to only use your brain to try and recall your DMI before looking for help from 'cheats'. First of all, try to recall the day before or after the day you've forgotten and perhaps work out which day it is in the week too. Often this will give you an idea of what you may have been up to or your likely whereabouts.

For people who take photos with their phones regularly, you can have a look at the photos taken on that day, as they might remind you of one of the day's events. If this still doesn't bring back your DMI, a 'cheat calendar' could be used. However, this should only be used if the previous two ways haven't helped you to locate your memory.

A 'cheat calendar'

All you need is a printed calendar (see 'Appendix') or a diary. You should only write down the *starting point* of each day. This could simply be the chosen place, with or without the symbol of that day's first event if required. It shouldn't be necessary to mark down every detail of each DMI because all you need is a hint to kickstart it. Once you have been reminded of how your DMI starts, your brain's engine should be ignited and you will move forward with ease. Most of the time you will realise that you do actually know the day like the back of your hand, you had just forgotten where to look.

If you write down all the details of the day and rely on it excessively, there really isn't any point forming a 'Mental Diary' at all, your 'cheat calendar' wouldn't be any different from an ordinary written diary!

You should only see this 'cheat calendar' as your safety net / last resort and only use it in a situation where you really, really struggle to remember. To prevent yourself from over-relying on it, try to not mark your first hint of a DMI on your cheat calendar until at least 1 week has past.

Creativity is memory's healthy buddy

Make your DMI as creative, ridiculous and weird as possible. This tends to stick in your brain a lot longer and more strongly. For instance, change the scale of things - an apple can be as big as a house; a train can be small enough to be held in your hands. Dramatise the scene - add party poppers if it is someone's birthday; set the place on fire if it is a hot day; let things go in slow motion if it is the most glorious day.

Additionally, try to use the different senses when remembering - make the flowers bloom with a sweet scent; let yourself hear deafening laughter; allow the taste of rotten cheese to linger on your tongue. The more vivid your mental image is, the stronger the day will be remembered. Remember, nothing is impossible in your imagination.

Keep each event close to your person

When forming a DMI, connect the symbols of events close to the month's person, as they are less likely to fade away over time.

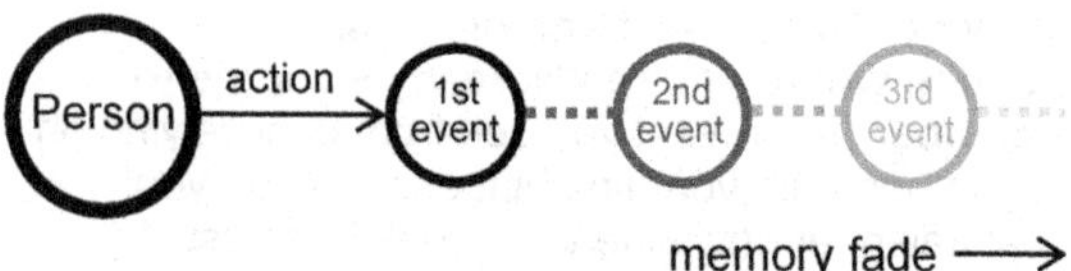

Below shows one example of how events can be kept close.

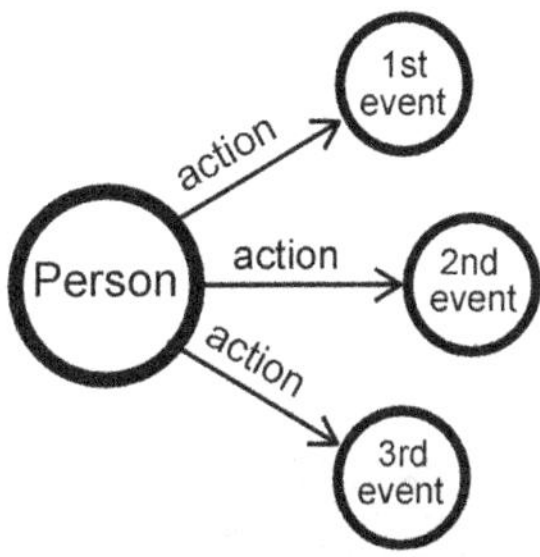

Of course, the direction of action can be from any angle.

Add-ons

Is it possible to add things to an existing day's DMI? The simple answer is yes! It may be that you wish to remember an event that your friend has experienced over the weekend but didn't tell you until the next day or week. Remembering significant details of your friends' lives is usually much appreciated, the same goes for your partner or family. Besides, this is one of the few ways you can prove to others that you do remember every day!

Travelling back in time

If you are interested and would like to go a step further, why not look back at old photos / videos that were taken before you started your Mental Diary? As long as they are dated, there is no limit to how long ago your Diary could start. However, if you do so you will have to revise the days in the same way we discussed in Step 5, in order for these 'new' old days to transfer to your long term memory.

Golden Memory, 2011

Examples of DMIs

Here are some examples of how to form Dynamic Mental Images (DMIs). Hopefully, this will assist you to better understand how this method works and will prevent any potential confusion. In case you wonder, they are all fictional events!

A quick reminder - there is no right or wrong way to form your Mental Diary. You may discover your own imaginative or logical way that suits you better. Note that the month's people and date's action words are again chosen from the example lists shown in Step 1 and 2.

Example 1:

On the morning of 31st March 2018, I went to the barbers for a haircut, so I could look nice for my date with Sarah in the afternoon. We walked through a pretty park and sat on a bench watching some beautiful swans gliding across the surface of the lake. The date started off very well until heavy rain drenched us from head to toe. Instead of staying out, I took her back to my home for some dry clothes and we spent the afternoon playing card games in the living room. Things went swimmingly and we ended up having our first kiss!

Chosen location = the bench in the park
March = Mickey Mouse
31st = scratch
Symbols of the important events = falling hair (haircut), floods (heavy rain), playing cards (card games), kiss with rose petals (first kiss), the bench in the park (walk in the park)

Your DMI:
On the park bench sits Sarah. Mickey Mouse is stressed as it floods up to knee level and therefore scratches Sarah's head so harshly that her hair starts to fall out. Sarah feels unwell and throws up a whole deck of playing cards. We still kiss as rose petals fall from the sky romantically.

Things to note:

1. A 'story' helps to form a stronger DMI by showing how the symbols link together. The more creative and bizarre it is, the more easily the day will be remembered.

2. Exaggeration / dramatisation of an event can help to create a more vivid scene making it easier to remember, hence the rain floods up to knee level and rose petals are added.

Reminiscence, 2016

Example 2:

On 21st December 2018, I went bowling with my usual group of friends from work: Harry, Ron and Hermione. We always hang out as a group of 4, but this time Harry brought a new friend called Ginny, whom I met for the first time. Afterwards, we went to the cinema and watched the movie 'Bugs Attack'.

Chosen location = the bowling lane
December = Winnie the Pooh
21st = slap
Symbols of the important events = bowling lane
(bowling), Harry (the usual group of friends), Ginny
(the new friend), a giant ant (watching Bugs Attack)

Your DMI:
In the bowling lane stands Harry and Ginny (visualise
a different Ginny who you have known for years).
They are holding a giant ant the size of a dog.
Winnie the Pooh slaps the ant out of their hands. The
ant spins and slides to the end of the lane and gets a
strike!

Things to note:

1. Only Harry was visualised (not Ron and Hermione),
    he is enough to remind you of the whole group.

2. As you have only just met Harry's friend, Ginny, her
    face is likely to be unfamiliar to you. It is much
    easier to use someone who you already know with
    the same name. This is also an effective way to
    remember new peoples' names. However, this
    ideally should not be a key person in your life in
    order to prevent confusion.Of course, once you
    have seen the new person enough times and have
    a stronger recognition of their face, you can swap
    in the real person.

About Time, 2012

Example 3:

On 16th August 2018, I decided to do some baking. In the kitchen, I prepared the mixture for a Belgian chocolate cake and put it in the oven with a timer set for 20 minutes. As the sun shone through the window, I realised how nice it was outside and saw that the grass needed cutting. I went out to mow the lawn, keeping in mind that I must return before the cake was ready. Just as I was walking back into the house after mowing the whole lawn in 15 minutes, my neighbour, Mary, asked me to help with moving a sofa from her car to her living room. She really appreciated my help and made me a nice cup of tea. Suddenly, the fire alarm went off from my house. I realised that I'd forgotten the cake. My house was filled with dark choking smoke. Luckily there was no fire and my cats were safe. Lesson learnt.

Chosen location = My Kitchen, Mary's living room
August = Buzz Lightyear
16th = push
Symbols of the important events = dark smoke (overcooked cake), lawnmower (mowing the lawn), kitchen at home (baking), Mary's living room (moving soda for her)

Your DMI:
While the oven is puffing out dark smoke, Buzz Lightyear pushes the lawnmower across the kitchen and escapes into Mary's living room, which is strangely attached to my house. There isn't even a wall between her living room and my kitchen.

Things to note:

1. The order of symbols doesn't have to match the sequence of events in real life. You will still be able to tell which happened first.

2. It is possible to use more than one location within the same DMI. This is also useful if one place holds many symbols already. However, it is important to keep the locations physically close together to minimise the chance of any disconnection in your DMI.

Example 4:

On 18th June 2018, I invited my group of close friends, Harry, Ron, Hermione and Ginny, to my house for a dinner party. Everyone enjoyed the civilised three-course meal in the dining room and the decent wine that accompanied it. After dinner, the smooth jazz playing in the background led us to start a graceful dance. However, after a certain level of alcohol intoxication, Ginny chose to perform a vigorous hip hop dance instead. She suddenly realised her stomach could no longer hold and started running for the sink in the kitchen. Unfortunately, she only made it halfway. The kitchen floor was artistically decorated with her three-course worth of vomitus.

Chosen location = the centre of my dining room
June = Arial
18th = levitate

Symbols of the important events = Harry (the whole group of my close friends), a glass of wine (3-course meal with wine), ~~vomitus (alcohol intoxication)~~, centre of my dining room (dancing, meal)

Your DMI:
Arial levitates Harry and a glass of wine in the centre of my dining room. They are spinning gracefully in midair with smooth jazz playing in the background. ~~Suddenly Harry falls down and lands face down in a big pile of pungent, acidic vomitus.~~

Things to note:

1. You will have noticed that the symbol of Ginny vomiting wasn't included in the DMI. This is because negative events don't always have to be remembered. One of the complaints from hyperthymestics is that they cannot forget negative experiences, however insignificant to other people. If you start to remember every little upsetting event in your life it could be very emotionally draining. Besides, I don't think your nearest and dearest would appreciate you remembering their every fault and the arguments you have had!

2. Overtime, you will generate DMIs that have a repeated location. In this example, I have used the centre of the dining room, instead of simply the dining room. This makes the location more specific. Another trick you can use is to change the angle of perception, e.g. see your DMI from above, from the side or behind. The less similar two DMIs' locations are, the less likely you will mix up the two days.

Alone, 2012

Example 5:

On 18th May 2018, I went to my Aunt Alice's house, to meet her newly adopted pets. Her four new puppies played happily with each other in the living room. On the same day, my eleven month old baby, Lucy, made her first step! On the sad side, the news reported a commercial plane tragically crashing at Cuba's international airport, killing more than one hundred people.

Chosen location = Alice's living room
May = Mr Incredible
18th = levitate
Symbols of the important events = a puppy contained in a *square* frame (4 puppies), Lucy with a massive foot (my baby started to walk), a cuboid block with a picture of a plane on one side (plane in Cuba)

Your DMI:
In my aunt's living room, Lucy with one massive foot stumbled and chased after a puppy in a square frame. Suddenly, a cuboid block (with a picture of a plane on its side) crashes through the roof. Mr Incredible levitates them all in the air to avoid the collision.

Things to note:

1. The number of objects (in this case, animals) could be marked with something representative. In this example, simple shapes were used - the number '4' was represented by a square because it has 4 sides. This is helpful especially when the quantity is great.

2. Names of places, objects or people can also be creatively represented. In this example, Cuba is similar to the word 'cube'. Therefore, a cuboid block (along with the picture of a plane) would be enough to make you think of Cuba. Regarding countries, you can also remember them using their flags. For instance, you can remember a plane painted in Cuba's flag's pattern instead.

Bobo (Author's dog), 2010

Example 6:

On 11th June 2018, I planned a nice walk for my first date with Georgia (it didn't work out with Sarah - *see Example 1!*). This walk was through a beautiful wood. We spent a great deal of time discussing the possible transplanetary colonisation of Mars.

Halfway through our walk it started to rain and so we took shelter in an empty tree house that we found. At first it was tranquil in the darkness, all we could hear was the echo of water droplets falling on the roof. However, after a little time, we started to hear a noise coming from the second floor above. As we were deciding whether to stay or leave, the stairs started to creak and a familiar face appeared from the shadows... It was Sarah and a friend who were clearly having the same idea as us! Awkward... We quickly left after a brief 'hello'.

Georgia and I were very compatible and she was interested to meet again.

Chosen location = the treehouse
June = Winnie the Pooh
11th = kick
Symbols of the important events = Mars
(conversation about colonising Mars), Sarah
(unexpectedly seeing her), treehouse (walk / rain)

Your DMI:
Winnie the Pooh stands at the top of the treehouse stairs, which are well-lit by fire torches. He kicks Mars down the stairs with such great force that it rolls and knocks Sarah out of the treehouse.

Things to note:

1. Virtual subjects, including a conversational topic, can be converted into an imaginary, tangible object. In this example, Mars was remembered as the actual physical planet (which also doesn't need in be to true scale).

2. Fire torches were added in the treehouse in the DMI to increase visibility, even though they didn't hold a major event. You will be surprised how much you will rely on your visual sense when recalling your DMIs.

Bude Farm Treehouse, 2016

So, this is it! I have tried my best to demonstrate how I write my Mental Diary. I hope that it all makes sense and that you have enjoyed learning about it. Now it is over to you… it is time for you to start your own Mental Diary, assuming you haven't already!

Brainstorm, 2011

Feedback from my Readers

At this point, I would like to note that all I have claimed in this book is entirely genuine and I really have made this method work. One limitation, however, is that there is no easy way to prove this. Even if I am quizzed and have my friends and family to verify my answers, it is still strictly speaking anecdotal. In order to support my technique, I need more interested people (on top of my father and a few close friends), like you, to attempt this method to test its efficacy.

Setting up and sustaining your Mental Diary does require a certain level of commitment, but it is definitely worth the 'pain' if you can at least try to reach the one month milestone. At this point I was able to clearly see the impact this technique had had on how I remembered my daily life and recognised what a tremendously positive experience it was. I'd like that to happen to you too.

And so, if you have made it to a month or beyond, well done! Does it work for you? What effects or changes do you think it has had on your life? Do you find it enjoyable and rewarding? Would you recommend others to do it too? I would love to hear your thoughts and will forever remember your comments!

Email address:
remember.every.day.of.your.life@gmail.com

Glossary

Dynamic Mental Image (DMI)
A short snapshot video that you mentally create every day. It shows you the major events associated with the date. See 'Your goal' and 'Step 4'.

Forgetting Curve
A hypothetical graph (created by Hermann Ebbinghaus) that shows the relationship between memory retention of learnt information and time.

Hermann Ebbinghaus (1850-1909)
A German psychologist who dedicated his life to the study of the nature of memory. His most well-known work includes the Forgetting Curve and Spacing Effect.

Memory Palace
Also known as the Method of Loci - a method first used by the Ancient Greeks and Romans. Its purpose is to accelerate the memorisation of a string of information in a mnemonic fashion, using either real or imaginary loci.

Memory sports
A competitive activity in which participants attempt to memorise and recall various forms of information under a time limit. Examples include remembering a shuffled deck of playing cards, randomly generated digits, binary digits, faces and names and texts.

Mental Diary
A method created by author, Sidney Chan, intended to create a diary using only the mind, so that one can recall the major events on any given date, as well as locating the specific date of a given event recorded in the Mental Diary.

Hidden Ideas, 2011

Sidney Chan

References

---

[1] Artofmemory.com. (2018). How to Build a Memory Palace - Memory Techniques Wiki. [online] Available at: https://artofmemory.com/wiki/How_to_Build_a_Memory_Palace [Accessed 1 May 2018].

[2] The World Memory Championships. (2018). About the sport - The World Memory Championships. [online] Available at: http://www.worldmemorychampionships.com/2015_wmc_china/ [Accessed 7 Jun. 2018].

[3] Jaeggi, S., Buschkuehl, M., Jonides, J. and Shah, P. (2011). Short- and long-term benefits of cognitive training. Proceedings of the National Academy of Sciences, [online] 108(25), pp.10081-10086. Available at: http://www.pnas.org/content/108/25/10081.short [Accessed 1 May 2018].

[4] Willis, S., Tennstedt, S., Marsiske, M., Ball, K., Elias, J., Koepke, K., Morris, J., Rebok, G., Unverzagt, F., Stoddard, A. and Wright, E. (2006). Long-term Effects of Cognitive Training on Everyday Functional Outcomes in Older Adults. JAMA, [online] 296(23), p.2805. Available at: https://www.ncbi.nlm.nih.gov/pmc/articles/PMC2910591/ [Accessed 1 May 2018].

[5] The Boy Who Can't Forget, (2012). [TV documentary] Channel 4 (World-wide): Studio Lambert.

[6] Henner, M. (2014). Total memory makeover. New York: Gallery Books.

---

[7] Meet the Man Who Can Remember Everything, (2016). [Radio Broadcast] The Takeaway: Public Radio International, WGBH and WNYC Studios.

[8] The Real Rain Man, (2006). [TV documentary] NHK: Focus Productions.

[9] Ebbinghaus, H. (1913). Memory: A contribution to experimental psychology. New York City: Teachers College, Columbia University.

Acknowledgements

First of all, I would like to thank a close friend of mine, Foo Yu Fang, who studied in the same year as me during our Vet degree. If he hadn't suggested that we go to the National History Museum and whilst there introduce me to the technique of 'Memory Palace', who knows how much longer it would have taken me to discover this new interest? For that I am very grateful.

I would also like to thank my family; my parents, who supported and encouraged me throughout my childhood and beyond, and opened the door to the many opportunities that the world has to offer; and Stanley, thank you for your contagious sense of fun and creativity, you are the best brother I could ever wish for.

Finally, I would like to take this opportunity to express my gratitude to my best friend, Emma, who continuously inspires me to be a better person. Only she understands and embraces my geekiness, especially how frequently I indulge in memorising random numbers and dates!

Appendix

Mon	Tues	Wed	Thur	Fri	Sat	Sun

Mon	Tues	Wed	Thur	Fri	Sat	Sun

Mon	Tues	Wed	Thur	Fri	Sat	Sun

Mon	Tues	Wed	Thur	Fri	Sat	Sun

Mon	Tues	Wed	Thur	Fri	Sat	Sun

Mon	Tues	Wed	Thur	Fri	Sat	Sun

Mon	Tues	Wed	Thur	Fri	Sat	Sun

Mon	Tues	Wed	Thur	Fri	Sat	Sun

Mon	Tues	Wed	Thur	Fri	Sat	Sun

Mon	Tues	Wed	Thur	Fri	Sat	Sun

Mon	Tues	Wed	Thur	Fri	Sat	Sun

Mon	Tues	Wed	Thur	Fri	Sat	Sun

Made in the USA
Monee, IL
07 July 2026

56546053R00046